fresh start

BIBLE STUDY

my new
identity
in Christ

julie baker

Victor® is an imprint of
Cook Communications Ministries, Colorado Springs, CO 80918
Cook Communications, Paris, Ontario
Kingsway Communications, Eastbourne, England

First printing 2003
Printed in the United States of America
1 2 3 4 5 6 7 8 9 10 Printing/Year 07 06 05 04 03

Senior Editor: Janet Lee
Editor: Susan H. Miller
Cover and Interior Design: Sandy Flewelling

Library of Congress Cataloging-in-Publication Data Submitted

fresh start

BIBLE STUDY

contents

let's talk "Christianese!"

When I was a high school senior, I was chosen to "suffer for Jesus" on a missions trip to JAMAICA! Well, somebody had to do it!

Since it was my first trip out of the United States, I was relieved when I discovered Jamaica was an English-speaking country—or at least that's what they told me.

On one of our first days of ministry, 14 of us—mostly musicians—piled into a white cargo van to visit and sing at some village churches in the mountains. To get there, our guide drove us straight through the inner-city area of Kingston. I was shocked at the poverty. People had actually taken up residence on street corners in refrigerator boxes.

As we neared one intersection, rather than speeding up to get through the turnabout, our guide pulled over and stopped. He honked the horn and immediately two very brown boys—in their early teens and with ear to ear smiles—sprang from a box and began talking excitedly to our guide. It was a language I had never heard before!

The guide introduced them to us, they joked around and slapped each other on the back a couple of times, then we were off to our engagement. Confused by what had just happened, I asked the guide what language they had spoken to him. His brow curved in disbelief. "Why, English, of course. But, it's the ghetto version. The words are all the same, they just say them differently." I'll say!

Christianity has a bit of its own lingo. Words that you've known all of your life to mean one thing take on a whole new dimension when they are spoken within the context of God's plan for our lives. In this study, we are going to analyze some of these terms so that you have a clear understanding about the foundation your new faith is being built upon. In a way, our "Christianese" language is a ladder that takes us from the first rung, which is Salvation, to the top rung, which is eternal life in heaven. Here are the steps we'll study:

Heaven

Holy Spirit

Prayer

Temptation

Faith

Repentance

Forgiveness

Salvation

Understanding the steps to eternity is just the beginning. We want to *go* from this study and *grow* in each area. We want to live the Christian life from the inside out. You will want to follow this study with the next two books in our Fresh Start series: *My New Relationships in Christ* and *My New Life in Christ*. Now let's delve into aspects of Salvation, our first step towards living a fulfilling life and gaining entry into eternity!

"Heavenly Father, may Your Word and will come to life for us in the Scriptures lessons in this study. Clear our minds so that we can focus on You. Please illuminate these truths so that they shine in our hearts as a beacon of hope! Amen."

salvation

a new start

A few years ago I received a phone call in the middle of a warm, humid summer afternoon. It was a mom from one of our car pools for church and school. At first she stammered around, talking small talk about nothing, really. I couldn't decipher all she was saying, or why. So, with a shot in the dark, I asked what was going on in her life. At that point, she began sobbing uncontrollably. Between gasps and wails, she confessed to me that she was calling me from a hospital room where she had been taken a few days before. I soon discovered that she had tried to take her own life but, thankfully, had failed at the attempt!

As she unfolded her story, she revealed a frayed tapestry woven from a painful life of childhood abuse, drug and alcohol addictions, and finally an affair that ended her marriage. At that point, she looked at the confusing pattern she had sewn for her life and determined there was nothing worth living for—so she decided to end it. She checked herself into a hotel, and then strolled up and down the river bank contemplating how to accomplish the deed.

She went back to her room where she consumed an entire bottle of wine. She fondled the photographs of each of her four children and told each of their images goodbye with a tender kiss. She then swallowed an entire bottle of prescription sedatives and waited to die.

Luckily, she was discovered the next day—barely alive—and rushed to the hospital where she lay in a coma for some time but eventually revived. As I cried with her and prayed with her over the phone, I turned to the Lord and said, "What can I say to this woman? Her life does seem to be such a mess! She's been the victim of hurt that wasn't her fault and then made some pretty bad decisions in her life. How can I comfort her and tell her there is hope? Lord, please give me a verse or a phrase or something that I can give to her to encourage her."

Immediately the words came to my mind: "Tell her that I am the Lord of new beginnings! No matter what the past, no matter what the hurt, I can wipe the slate of her past clean and give her a new beginning!"

This woman held on with faith to this new beginning from the Lord, and today we see in her what happens when we allow God to weave His love into our lives. What results is a beautiful pattern—all because we put our trust in Him.

A new beginning in Christ is called *Salvation.* Salvation can be defined as the act of being saved from destruction or catastrophe. In this lesson we are going to discover how salvation through Jesus Christ frees us from the grip of sin and allows us to be woven into the image of Christ.

bible study

In order to fully understand our need for salvation and how to receive it, we must first understand what sin is and where it leads us.

Read Genesis 2:15–17 and Genesis 3:1–24.

What commandment did God give to Adam?

"... You must not eat from the tree of knowledge of good and evil?..."

What would be the consequences for disobeying God?

Your relationship with God will be over.

What happened after Adam and Eve disobeyed God?

Their perfect fellowship with God was changed, separated They felt shame, fear. They recognize their sin, they hide from it.

Based on what you learned from this story, how would you define sin?

Notice how crafty the Serpent is in these references. One question, "Did God really say ... ?" changed the course of

put on the helmet of salvation

In Ephesians 6:13–17, the apostle Paul instructs us to put on the full armor of God: the Belt of Truth, the Breastplate of Righteousness, the Shield of Faith, and Sword of the Spirit, AND THE HELMET OF SALVATION.

You ask, "Why do I need armor?" The answer: Every human being is a soldier involved in spiritual warfare. Satan will do everything possible to render you disabled— or better yet, destroyed. He will use subtle lies to discourage you, interject insignificant circumstances to take your focus off of God, and nibble away at your weakest areas.

You ask, "Is there a solution?" The answer: Yes! God always makes provision for our protection. One of the most important pieces of armor for us to wear is the Helmet of Salvation. The Helmet covers our mind, keeping it from fearful thoughts, doubts, and temptation. Go ahead! Put it on ... it won't even mess up your hair!

history by placing doubt in the mind of the woman. Doubt is a powerful tool in the hands of our enemy, and when it causes us to doubt God's truth, we begin sliding on a slippery slope! It's important for us to discern God's truth from Satan's lies so that we don't end up like Eve.

To understand better the reality of our sinful condition, read the following verses and make a note about what each one tells you about sin.

Psalm 51:5

Isaiah 59:2

Romans 3:23

Romans 5:12–14

Now read Hebrews 4:15–16 and 1 John 1:8–9.
Has anyone lived without sinning? Explain.

What happens if we deny our own sin?

What happens if we confess our sin?

Be encouraged, because God is always a step ahead of humans. He has always had a plan for us to fellowship with Him, and in His mercy, we can take some simple steps towards reconciliation with Him!

Read Romans 6:23.
What is the result of sin?

How do we gain eternal life?

For more about God's gift of eternal life, read John 3:16–18; 34–36, John 14:6, 1 Peter 3:18, and 1 John 4:10.
What did God do so that we could have eternal life?

What does God want us to do so we can have eternal life?

What happens to those who reject the Son?

What motivated God to send Jesus?

Why is it important that Christ "died for sins once for all"?

Now read Romans 1:1–6.

How do we know that Jesus is the Son of God?

How does Jesus' resurrection from the dead show power over sin?

Based upon the Scriptures we've read, how would you define salvation?

Now read on to see how you can claim Jesus' salvation as your own and what that could mean in your life.

my plan

The steps to receiving salvation by accepting Christ as your personal Savior are so easy that a child can understand and receive Him; yet so profound that scholars for centuries have studied the Scriptures with great enthusiasm and amazement.

Just keep in mind the three "A's" of becoming a Christian:

- *Acknowledge Him as Lord and Savior*

- *Ask Him to forgive your sins*

- *Allow Him to enter your heart*

Which of the verses we studied in this lesson best helped you understand the meaning of salvation? Copy that verse here:

Once we've taken these first three steps on our journey, we become new—what the Bible terms "reborn." Second Corinthians 5:17 tells us that "if anyone is in Christ, he is a new creation; the old has gone, the new has come!"

Explain in your own words what you think 2 Corinthians 5:17 means:

If you have not yet accepted Jesus Christ as your personal Savior, and you would like to, just repeat this simple prayer after me: "Lord, I acknowledge You as my Lord and Savior and ask You to forgive me of my sins. Please come into my life and help me to build a personal relationship with You."

Congratulations! You have just become a member of a family—God's family. And you've received a supernatural gift; one where you've been cleansed from your sins and been forgiven for them. So, what does the experience of forgiveness really mean? That will be the focus of our next lesson!

"Father, thank You for making it possible for us to enter into a relationship with You. Thank You for forgiving us our sins and giving us a fresh start at living a new life with You! Amen."

forgiveness

a new path to freedom

Freedom. Perhaps this isn't the word you would have chosen to accompany the word *forgiveness*. Frankly, it's the best term that I can think of to describe what forgiveness is all about and where it leads.

After one of our TimeOut for Women! conferences a few years ago, I received a letter from a woman in her mid-fifties. Her first comments were, "I'm finally free!" As she told her story, she revealed that she and all of her 11 siblings had been victims of their father's childhood abuse. That abuse shrouded her like a dark cloud all of her life as she struggled with bitterness, low self-esteem, and fear—because she could not forgive him.

No one on our platform that day had spoken about the need to forgive, but the Holy Spirit so convicted her that she laid her hurt at Jesus' feet. In realizing how much her Heavenly Father had forgiven her of her shortcomings and wrongdoings, she realized that she needed to forgive her earthly father. And the result? "I'm finally free!"

We're going to delve into three different aspects of forgiveness in this lesson. The first will be to come to an understanding of the need for God's forgiveness in order to be freed from the penalty of our sins. Some would argue that this is the only necessary type of forgiveness—accepting God's. Not true! If we want to grow in our relationship with Christ, we must also grant forgiveness!

So, the second discussion on forgiveness will deal with the importance of forgiving others and what those benefits are to us as well as to the people we forgive. Mind you, forgiving others is not a choice. We *must* forgive if we are to follow the commandments of Jesus. A side benefit is that, like the woman at our conference, it frees our focus and energy to be positioned on God, not self or the ones who hurt us.

Finally, we will take a look at how being able to forgive ourselves frees us from obsessing about past mistakes and brings relief from overwhelming guilt. Again, that crafty trickster, Satan, wants to deceive us into thinking that because we're not good enough, God won't forgive us, so we shouldn't forgive ourselves. Don't fall into that trap! If we look long and painstakingly at the past, we miss what God has for us in the future.

Throughout His ministry, Jesus often spoke on the importance of forgiveness, but no demonstration was as poignant as the scene of His own death on the cross. Even then, as He took upon Himself the sins of the world, suffering physically as well as in His spirit, He prayed, "Father forgive them, for they do not know what they are doing" (Luke 23:34). Jesus has set before us the supreme example of finding freedom through forgiveness ... freedom from sin's penalty, freedom from bitterness, and freedom from guilt.

bible study

Our new identity in Jesus Christ is a lifetime process of becoming more like Him. As we observe His perfect ways, we want to model His teachings and behavior. The Bible is very clear about our need to receive God's forgiveness and commands us to show like forgiveness to those around us!

God's Forgiveness
Read Psalm 103:10–12.

How do these verses describe God's forgiveness?

He loves much, he forgives us.

Read 2 Chronicles 7:11–12 and 1 John 1:9.

What must we do to receive God's forgiveness? List several things.

To admit our sin and transform humble ourselves

Read Matthew 9:6; Mark 3:28–29; Ephesians 2:8–9.

*Who has authority to forgive sins, and is there any sin too
great to be forgiven?*

*Son of God, Jesus.
Everything, except blasphemia.*

Can we earn forgiveness? Explain.

*No, It's free. Believe, trust in
God.*

*(God's
Riches
at
Christ
expense.
Grace)*

Forgiving Others

Many new Christians enjoy the freedom they find in
God's forgiveness, but then seem to stagnate. Often this is
because they are caught in the trap of unforgiveness towards
another. They cannot escape this trap without turning to
God for help! Even a simple prayer such as, "Lord, I know I
need to forgive this one who hurt me so. In Your strength,
Lord, I forgive" has freed many. As you study the following
Scriptures, you will discover that granting forgiveness is
more than a nice gesture; we are *commanded* to.

**What does the Bible say about forgiving others in these
passages?**

Mark 11:24–25

Luke 6:37

Matthew 6:14–15

Matthew 18:21–22

Ephesians 4:29–32.

Read Luke 17:3–4; Matthew 18:15–17
What should we do when others sin against us?

Forgiving Ourselves

We're pretty tough on ourselves sometimes, aren't we? We look back at the mistakes we've made and wonder how we can ever live with ourselves. This is right where Satan would love to keep us. Again, we need to focus on God's truth: Once we've asked for and been granted forgiveness of our sins from God, He acknowledges them no more!

Read Hebrews 10:22–23.
Is it possible to forgive ourselves of our sin and failures? How?

Read Ephesians 2:4–9.

Based on these verses, how would you define "grace"?

Why is grace so important in accepting and understanding forgiveness?

To understand more clearly the scope of God's forgiveness, we must return to that recurring theme, sin. Our need for forgiveness results from committing sin. Jesus faced a challenging situation as the religious leaders of that day tried to trick Him. They were hoping to snag Him by setting up a situation where Jesus would have to break either Jewish or Roman law. Either way, they'd have His throat, so they thought. Jesus, however, used this embarrassing situation to teach us several truths about sin and forgiveness.

Read John 8:3–11.

What truth did Jesus emphasize when He challenged anyone without sin to throw the first stone?

What happens when we try to point out someone else's sin?

How did Jesus respond to the woman's sin? What were His instructions to her?

Does this story reveal anything to you about your own sin and your relationship with Jesus Christ? If so, what?

Sometimes we dig an emotional grave for ourselves by dwelling too long and too hard on our past sin and the guilt we feel as a result. It is natural that after asking for salvation and receiving forgiveness that there will be a time when we look at what we've been and what we've done with shame and guilt. For a time, this is healthy. For a prolonged season, it can be harmful.

Remember that God wants us to live in grace not guilt! A prolonged time of "looking back" can lead to some unhealthy issues in our lives.

List some possible consequences of looking back and not moving forward in your Christian experience. Let me help with one possible adverse outcome: depression.
Can you think of others?

what is the "unpardonable sin?"

Acts 2:21 emphatically tells us that, "... *everyone* who calls on the name of the Lord will be saved." Mark 3:28-29, however, seems to contradict this statement: "I tell you the truth, all the sins and blasphemies of men will be forgiven them. But whoever blasphemes against the Holy Spirit will never be forgiven; he is guilty of an eternal sin."

To understand Jesus' statement, we need to first define what blasphemy is. Blasphemy against the Holy Spirit takes place if a person *attributes to Satan* a deed done by Jesus through the power of God's Spirit. This has come to be known as the "unpardonable sin."

The point is not whether God is willing to forgive all sins, but that anyone who would commit such a sin is so hard-hearted that he has put himself beyond the possibility of *repentance*. Forgiveness only takes place when we ask for it.

How does dwelling too much on past sin inhibit our spiritual growth?

Can it affect us physically? Explain.

When we are tempted to look back at our past sin in an unforgiving way, what should we do?

When we are tempted to bring up past sins—our own or someone else's—how does that affect our relationship with Jesus and with each other?

my plan

Perhaps you've studied this lesson and have never come before the Lord to confess your sin and ask for forgiveness. There is no better time than now!

In your own words, explain why you need God's forgiveness.

Now ask for God's forgiveness. Simply bow your head and in humbleness acknowledge that you have sinned and are asking God, through the work of Jesus Christ on the cross, for forgiveness. There is nothing you can do to earn forgiveness; it is a *free* gift! However, to demonstrate your thankfulness and love to the Lord Jesus for granting you forgiveness, you will want to make choices in your life that reflect God's will for you.

When you read about forgiveness, you may find that certain names or situations come to your mind. Times when someone hurt you and never apologized. Times when you know you hurt someone else and never apologized to them, or tried to justify your actions. Times when you knew you were doing something wrong.

Confession is a key part of seeking forgiveness. Think for a moment about people you need to forgive. You may want to write their names here.

Don't forget to forgive yourself! You are the one who knows if you've done something you haven't forgiven yourself for—or haven't accepted God's forgiveness. If God can forgive you—and He does—you can forgive yourself.

One thing you may be asking is "Do Christians sin?" First John 1:8–9 tells us that we, by nature, are sinners, but assures us that we will not lose our salvation. It says, "If we claim to be without sin, we deceive ourselves and truth is not in us. If we confess our sins, he is faithful and just and will forgive our sins ... ."

Is confessing enough? True confession is followed by what we call repentance. If I continually sin and confess that sin to the Lord, I continue to hammer the nails into His hands on the cross. Yes, I'm forgiven, but I am not allowing the Holy Spirit to guide my life. When I repent of my sin, I stop my sinful activity and allow God to have power over my life.

"Lord, I confess to You my sin and ask that You give me the power to truly repent. Amen."

repentance

a new walk

I walked into the classroom I had been assigned as a substitute teacher. As I entered the room, a ninth grade male student was hopping from one desk top to the next. I quickly figured out that his destination was the wall clock. Sure enough, he took off the cover and moved the minute hand ahead by about 10 minutes, then replaced the cover.

By this time, silence permeated the room as the class realized who I must be and what I had just witnessed. This was my first introduction to Mike.

Oh, we would meet up many times after that since we attended the same church. We even ended up on the same three-week mission trip to Barcelona during the 1992 Olympics. He broke every rule in the book, including helping himself to the complimentary alcoholic beverages on the plane ride over and dumping a garbage can filled with water over the music team during practice. It's amazing no one was electrocuted that day! Anyway, he was the kid you couldn't hate because he was so lovable, but he was so frustrating that you just wanted to wring his neck!

After each mischievous deed, he would get this pitiful look in his eyes and apologize for his infraction. Each time he promised he had learned his lesson and turned over a new leaf. He seemed repentant each time, yet I knew that it wasn't heartfelt because his misbehaving continued.

He vanished off to college, and four years later we literally crashed into each other in a stairwell at church. "Mrs. Baker!," he shouted, "I want you to meet my wife." Wife? Imagine that! Then he said something I'll never forget. "Remember how I told you I had repented and really changed? Well, guess who's preaching the Wednesday night service?" I flipped to the schedule in the bulletin and there was Wednesday's sermon topic and his name next to it! His behavior proved to me that he had truly repented. He had stopped practicing the old hurtful conduct, done a 180, and truly changed. Today he is a remarkable young man—one whom I admire, respect, and can learn much about the Bible from!

Our conduct says a lot about our heart, doesn't it? Our behavior will always underscore our value system and beliefs. Like Mike, we may acknowledge and be sorry for what we've said or done, but true repentance takes place when our actions are consistent with our words.

Repentance in the life of a Christian is a very important element. Yes, we will all continue to sin in some degree, but as one of my spiritual mentors once taught me to ask, are we sinning less today than yesterday? If we are, we are experiencing spiritual growth. But if we fail at times along the way, God has opened up to us the door of repentance allowing us to confess that sin and change our behavior. We are a kind of work in progress, standing before a merciful God who is willing to overlook our flaws when we come to Him for help!

bible study

It's possible to come into a personal relationship with Jesus Christ, but then feel as if we stall in our growth process. Often, sin keeps us from moving on in our spiritual journey. The Bible gives us excellent instruction in how to come to grips with this pitfall so that we can climb up and move out!

Read Genesis 6:5–8.

How would you describe the affect of a sinful world on the heart of God?

Read Isaiah 30:15; Jeremiah 15:19; Ezekiel 18:21, 30–32.

What benefits do we reap through the process of repentance?

Read Psalm 51.

What tone or attitude does David establish in his prayer?

To which character trait of God does David appeal?

Who has David really sinned against?

What truth about repentance does David reveal to us in verses 6 and 12?

What does God value over sacrifice?

In our faith journey towards repentance, keep in mind that we are not walking this road on our own. When we pray for the Holy Spirit to reveal our sin, He will faithfully point it out. Through the *power* of the Holy Spirit we have supernatural ability to change our sinful actions.

Read the following Scripture verses, which describe components of repentance, and explain each in a short phrase.

Matthew 27:3

Matthew 18:3; Luke 13: 3, 5

Luke 15:7, 10

Matthew 3:8; Luke 3:8

Mark 1:15

Acts 2:38

Acts 3:19

Romans 2:4

2 Corinthians 10:7

Read Acts 26:20.

Give examples of outward deeds that signify inner repentance.

Matthew 12:34 states a profound truth about the connection between a heart of true repentance and its outward affect: "For out of the overflow of the heart the mouth speaks." When we continually take inventory of our iniquities, confess them, and repent, this has a profound impact on the way we live our lives and how we affect the lives of others.

Read Luke 7:36–50.

What does this story reveal about the power of repentance?

hyssop

The hyssop, part of the marjoram family, is known for its mint aroma. In Jewish history, the hyssop is significant because it was used in purification ceremonies (Leviticus 14:4–7), and was dipped in blood, then sprinkled upon the door posts at the first Passover (Exodus 12:22).

King David's prayer of repentance also refers to the hyssop. In Psalm 51:7 he says, "Cleanse me with hyssop, and I will be clean; wash me, and I will be whiter than snow."

Fast-forward to the New Testament where John 19:28–30 describes Jesus' last moments on the cross. Jesus accepts wine vinegar offered on hyssop. Hyssop ushered in the first Passover, and hyssop was in the last cup Jesus would drink as He spilled His blood to cover our sin.

This hyssop, or marjoram, spice can still today serve as a reminder to us of Jesus' cleansing power over sin. I would encourage you to add it to soup and meat recipes and as you do, bow your head with me and repent of any sins committed against God.

How do the woman's inner changes affect her outward choices?

What attitudes does she adopt as a result her repentance?

Can you sense a difference in your thoughts and actions since repenting? If so, how?

Although the "sinful woman" had made decisions that led to her sinful lifestyle, there are times when someone else sin against us. The Bible makes it clear how we are to respond so that we do not sin against the one who has offended us.

Read Luke 17:3–4.

How should we respond when someone sins against us?

How did Jesus illustrate this truth to Simon Luke 7:36–50?

One of the most beautiful stories of sin and repentance is that of King David and his sin of committing murder and adultery.

Read 2 Samuel 11:1–17, 26–27; 12:7–13.
What is David's attitude at the beginning of the story?

What is David's attitude at the end of the story?

To wrap up the story of David's repentance, read Psalm 32:1–5. Some scholars believe that this was written at the same time David wrote Psalm 51, around the time he met Bathsheba.

What strikes you about this passage written by David?

How does this encourage you in your own walk?

Although few of us have committed a murder to get away with adultery, sin has no "degrees" in God's eyes, and we are no better than David. Yet God loved David so much that He often called him "a man after my own heart." That's because of David's willingness to admit his failure and come before God in repentance—with a changed mind and behavior. Like David, we stumble at times. Sometimes our sins have far-reaching consequences. But God is there with an outstretched hand ready to let us hold on to Him. The forgiveness David received can be ours, too. What an encouragement!

my plan

Visualize that moment when the larva bursts forth as a beautiful butterfly. This image illustrates the idea of repentance. A
metamorphosis takes place when there is a change of shape.
The word repentance comes from the same root word in the
Greek: metanoia. Repentance refers to *a change of mind.*

Think of some other images of a complete change of
mind and write them here:

True repentance results in more than just a change of
mind, however. Repentance takes place when there is a
change of life direction. It's not enough that we believe in
Jesus and the forgiveness of sins (even the demons do that);
our choices and decisions must now reflect that we have
turned from our wicked ways to do God's will. Repentance
reflects a transformation within us that spills over to our
actions.

Perhaps you've made a statement of faith in Christ Jesus and are assured that your sins are forgiven. However, there may yet be some areas where true repentance needs to take place. List several areas of your life where you know you need repentance. These might be behaviors you know God wants you to change, attitudes that you know are wrong, or desires or goals that you have not surrendered to God's control for the future.

Now pray over the list and lay these things at the cross of Jesus. Ask Him to not only help you in the change of your mind, but in the change of your decisions and choices.

You cannot make changes in your choices and decisions in your own strength! Only the divine power of the Holy Spirit can do that. Choose a Bible verse that will remind you of this truth. Write it on an index card and put it somewhere in your home or office where you will see it several times a day.

"Lord, thank You for helping me repent and change my ways. Now, please help me grow in my faith. Amen."

faith

a new reason to trust

He made his way into the kitchen, whistling and opening one cupboard after another until he discovered the spices. This is interesting, I thought. The only things my husband can cook are scrambled eggs and French toast.

After lifting several containers and reading the labels, apparently he found what he was looking for. He opened the cap and tapped something into his hand. "Got any tape?"

"In my office."

He scuffed through the living room into my office and tore off a piece of tape. On his way back through the living room, he stopped before me and held out the tape to show me he had doubled it over to hold a small mustard seed. He then quoted Jesus' words found in Matthew 17:20: "... if you have faith as small as a mustard seed, you can say to this mountain, 'Move from here to there' and it will move. Nothing will be impossible for you."

That small piece of tape with the mustard seed in it is still attached to the inside of my husband's briefcase as a constant reminder of the fact that with just the smallest amount of faith "nothing will be impossible" for us.

Faith has to do with what we believe and put our trust in. When we make a commitment to Jesus, our faith may seem small and weak, but when we remember the mustard seed, we take heart. You see, in Jesus' time, the mustard seed was the smallest seed known. Yet when planted on fertile ground and given the right atmosphere, the mustard plant would grow over 15 feet tall! We may possess just the smallest amount of faith that we are willing to place in the power and presence of Jesus Christ, but over time, as we see promises fulfilled and experience His grace in our lives, our faith begins to grow.

An active, growing faith reaches its roots deep into the Word of God and branches out. It points its upper blossoms towards heaven and bears fruit. Faith is not a one-time activity, but a continuing process. You may have expressed it for the first time when making a commitment to Jesus Christ, but you will find that you must practice faith daily if you wish to grow deeper and broader in your relationship to Christ.

Faith is based upon one thing and one thing alone—Jesus Christ. We must trust not only in the *power* of Jesus, but in his *character*. He has the power to do anything we ask, but our request may not be God's will or in our best interest. When we pray in faith, we know he can move that mountain, but we trust that if he doesn't, there is good reason.

The Bible is loaded with true-life stories that depict men and women growing in their faith. For us, this is evidence of the power and character of God through His son Jesus Christ. Faith is believing that what God has promised will be so. There will be times when it just won't look like it, but we must be persistent in trusting and believing. And when we are, "nothing will be impossible!"

bible study

In Hebrews 11, the writer gives a beautiful definition of faith and cites examples of people who lived by faith in the Old Testament. He is speaking to first century Jews, so he refers to Scriptures they readily understood and accepted. He makes the connection that these Old Testament believers accepted God's promises by faith, just as present-day Jews must accept by faith that Jesus Christ fulfilled the prophesies as the promised Messiah.

Read Hebrews 11.

How does the writer of Hebrews define faith?

Is it possible to please God without faith? Explain.

Let's do some Bible surfing and study a few of the Old Testament references in Hebrews 11.

Read about Enoch in Genesis 5:18–24.

How did Enoch show faith, and how did God reward him?

Read about Noah in Genesis 6:9–22; 7:1–10, 24; 8:13–22.

How did Noah show faith, and how did God reward him?

Read about Abraham in Genesis 12:1–5; 15:1–6; 17:15–22; 21:1–7. (Also, Romans 4:18–25.)

How did Abraham show faith, and how did God reward him?

Read just one incident in the life of Moses as described in Exodus 12:1–30.

How did Moses show faith, and how did God reward him?

Read about Rahab in Joshua 2:1–24; 6:22–25; Matthew 1:1, 5.

How did Rahab show faith, and how did God reward her?

Refer again to Hebrews 11:39–40.

Are we always rewarded for our faith?

What is that "something better" God has planned for those who have faith?

We've taken a look at the lives of just a few of the faithful mentioned in the Bible. Their lives inspire us to live our lives based upon faith in God and provide proof that God is always faithful to us in fulfilling His promises.

The Bible also has examples of nations and people who lacked faith and the consequences of their unbelief. Some of them, like us, were believers! Others, however, no matter the miracles from God and His direct connection with them, turned a hard heart and refused to trust Him. The outcome and result for them was disappointment and ultimately estrangement from God.

faith and miracles

Many times throughout Scripture, we see a correlation between faith and miracles. When Jesus healed a woman who had been bleeding for 12 years (Mark 5:34), He praised her by saying, "Daughter, your faith has healed you." When a Roman Centurion came to Jesus asking Him to heal his servant, Jesus exclaimed to His followers, "I tell you the truth, I have not found anyone in Israel with such great faith"(Matthew 8:10). When two blind men follow Jesus into the house where He was staying He asks, "Do you believe that I am able to do this?" They respond that they do, so Jesus says, "According to your faith will it be done to you"(Matthew 9:29).

Why did Jesus perform miracles? Was it so that it would relieve human suffering? Probably. But the real reason was so that God the Father would be glorified and that we would believe in Him.

Read Deuteronomy 1:26–36; Psalm 95:7–11; Hebrews 3:7–19.

How did the Children of Israel express their lack of faith in God?

What were the consequences?

45

How can we avoid the hardening of our hearts?

Read John 6:60–69.

Why did many of Jesus' disciples desert Him?

What do you think might have caused them to walk away?

For what reason did the 12 stay?

How can this apply to our lives today?

Let's wind up our discussion on faith with some additional biblical examples that can encourage us when we struggle.

Read James 2:14–26.

What points does James make regarding faith and works?

Can you list several areas in your life where you can better demonstrate your faith through your deeds and actions?

Is believing that God exists enough to demonstrate faith? How does James emphasize this point?

Read Matthew 8:23–27; John 12:42–43; John 14:22–33; 1 John 1:15–21.

What effect does fear have on our faith?

What causes fear?

How can we rid ourselves of fear?

Read Mark 9:17–27.

How does Jesus respond to the father's statement "... if you can do anything, have pity on us"?

Write out and memorize the father's response.

Is it a sin to believe, yet still have unbelief? Explain.

How does Jesus respond to our unbelief?

my plan

Faith is more than a one-time experience. As we grow in our friendship with Jesus Christ, we find that each day our trust is tested. Things may appear to be headed in the opposite direction from what we know God has promised, but we must remain constant in our belief that God is in control. As the writer of Hebrews said, "Faith is being sure of what we hope for and certain of what we do not see" (Hebrews 11:1).

List some times or situations in your life when things did not go in the direction you expected.

Looking back, can you see God's hand? Explain.

Faith is more than believing that God is God. Faith is putting our whole being into the hands and control of Jesus Christ, trusting Him with every aspect of our lives. The outward expression of our faith results in works that please and glorify the Lord.

As Peter evidenced, we may lapse into fear or doubt at times. Even the most experienced and knowledgeable believer will occasionally lack in faith. One of the best ways to fight the temptation to be discouraged is to pray the Word of God. The following are promises that you can memorize and be encouraged by when your faith is tested. Look up the verses and jot down a key thought next to the reference. Then write out each promise on an index card and put them in places around your home where you will see them often. Read them each day this week until you commit them to memory. You will be amazed at the way these words will encourage and protect you!

- *1 Peter 5:7*

- *James 1:12*

- *Hebrews 10:23*

- *Hebrews 11:6*

- *Philippians 4:19*

- *Ephesians 2:8*

- *Romans 3:22*

- *Romans 8:28*

- *Matthew 28:20b*

"Thank You, Jesus, for being with me always! Amen."

temptation

a new source of strength

Years ago, comedian Flip Wilson created a female character named Geraldine. When caught doing something a
little shady, her usual quip was, "The Devil made me do it!" We
all laugh at this because deep down inside we wish that we
could all blame our shortcomings and bad choices on someone
or something other than ourselves. The truth is, although we
may be influenced and "tempted" by Satan, we are agents of
free choice and we can decide whether to listen to that voice,
or to that of the living Word of God, Jesus Christ.

Those who do not have a personal relationship with
Jesus Christ give in to temptations each day. Many make
moral choices based upon whether it "feels good" or whether
they can get away with it. I recently heard a professional
administrator brag about the fact that he was able to rig his
computer system to cast multiple on-line votes for a particular issue. In fact, he cast over 400 votes, thus swaying the
decision in his favor. Little does he know that he is just a
pawn in the hands of Satan, carrying out unfair and illegal

acts like a puppet on a string. As long as his side won and he didn't get caught, he believes it must be okay. His sense of right and wrong is skewed because he doesn't know the Author of Truth.

On the other hand, for those of us who have a personal relationship with Jesus Christ, we become acutely aware of what is right and what is wrong. As we grow in our faith and search the Scriptures, we recognize the above act as lying and cheating—a basic principle addressed by the Ten Commandments.

So, not only are we aware of what is acceptable to God and what isn't, but we are given power to resist the temptation to do wrong. Geraldine would have been more accurate if she'd said, "The Devil tempted me to do it." Each of us faces temptation on a regular—sometimes daily—basis.

When we are tempted, how should we respond? Are we guilty of sinning when we are tempted? How do we resist temptation? What should we do if we give into temptation?

God knew that Satan would consistently be challenging us with people and situations that would make it difficult for us to remain faithful to God's Word. That's why he recorded in the Bible the life stories of real-life men and women who faced the same issues we still deal with today.

Let's take a look at some Bible stories that will help us more fully understand what temptation is and ways to resist it. By reading about people who made both good and bad choices and evaluating the results of their actions, we can learn from their mistakes and strengthen our resolve to be strong in the Lord.

bible study

The Old Testament refers more to "trials and testings" than to temptations. In each testing, God gives an opportunity for His people to show their trust and faithfulness to Him. Some fail the test miserably, such as Adam and Eve, but others come out victorious in their obedience to God. Let's take a look at the testing of Joseph and Job in the Old Testament and the temptation of Jesus in the New Testament.

Read about an incident in the life of Joseph in Genesis 39.
What is your general impression of Joseph?

How would you characterize Potiphar's wife?

What do you suppose prompted her to be so persistent in pursuing Joseph?

What kept Joseph from giving into this temptation?

What are the initial consequences of his resistance?

What are the long-term consequences of his faithfulness? (Read also Genesis 41:41–45.)

How does Joseph's experience encourage and inspire you?

Read Job 1:1–12.

How does Satan receive access to Job?

What does this tell us about God's power versus Satan's power?

What was it about Job that irritated Satan so much?

Read the devil's temptation of Christ in Matthew 4:1–12; Luke 4:1–13; Mark 1:12–13.

What is the significance of the three things Satan tempts Jesus about?

How does Jesus respond?

What does this teach us about how to resist temptation?

Why is it significant that Jesus was tempted? (Read also Hebrews 2:17–18.)

While Satan may use temptation to get us to sin, God will often allow the temptation to test to our obedience to Him. We must remember that God is in complete control of the universe and that Satan is also bound by what God will allow. We can take heart when faced with difficulty because we know that "... in all things God works for the good of those who love him" (Romans 8:28), and "when he has tested me, I will come forth as gold" (Job 23:10).

All of us are subject to being tempted, but we have been given a greater power that can resist temptation. One way to begin the journey of overcoming temptation is to recognize what things constitute sin in our lives.

Read Exodus 20:3–17. Write down each commandment, then write a "shall" statement that paraphrases the idea.

Example:

1st Commandment: "You shall have no other gods before me." (Exodus 20:3)

My paraphrase: "I shall put God before my job, my hobbies, and my pleasures. He will be #1 in my life."

2nd Commandment:
My paraphrase:

3rd commandment:
My paraphrase:

4th Commandment:
My paraphrase:

5th Commandment:
My paraphrase:

6th Commandment:
My paraphrase:

7th Commandment:
My paraphrase:

8th Commandment:
My paraphrase:

9th Commandment:
My paraphrase:

10th Commandment:
My paraphrase:

We've already discovered a couple of ways to stand up to temptation. Joseph removed himself from the situation; Christ quoted Scripture. Read Matthew 26:41, Mark 14:38, and Luke 22:40, 46 and describe another way to ward off temptation.

James 4:7 is gives more good advice when it comes to facing temptation. What is it?

Read James 1:12–17; 1 Corinthians 10:12–13; Hebrews 4:14–16; Ephesians 4:25–27; 1 Peter 5:2–9; Revelation 12:7–12; Revelation 20:7–10.

Is it possible for God to tempt us? Explain.

shedding light on the "prince of darkness"

2 Corinthians 11:14 tells us that "Satan himself masquerades as an angel of light." Perhaps this is the most sinister of Satan's qualities, since the most dangerous deception is one that resembles truth.

Satan is clever and intelligent, yet does not possess limitless power as does God. He is subject to God's restrictions. There are times when Satan has been allowed to afflict God's people, however as in Job 1:7-12, Satan is restricted by God. It was spiritual warfare that delayed an answer to prayer in Daniel 10. Yet in each case, God was and is the ultimate victor and receives glory and honor through the victory.

How can we keep from being tempted and deceived? 1 John 4:1-4 gives us the answer. We must "test the spirits." We must pray for the ability to discern God's truth from Satan's lies.

Can God be tempted? Explain.

Has anyone ever been exempt from temptation?

How does God help us in our times of temptation?

What kinds of behavior help defeat Satan?

What is Satan's ultimate destiny?

my plan

What areas of your life irritate Satan? These may be his first targets for temptation. On the other hand, Satan may be delighted with some of your habits, and his job is simply to tempt you not to change them!

List here several areas in your life that you recognize as being susceptible to temptation. These may be habits, time commitments, or relationships.

1.

2.

3.

4.

5.

In our own strength, resisting temptation is easier said than done. The good news is that we don't have to resist temptation in our own strength. List here some of the ways God helps you resist temptation. These may be people you're accountable to, Bible verses, songs—anything that expresses God's faithfulness to you so you can be faithful to Him.

1.

2.

3.

4.

5.

What is the most valuable lesson you've learned from this study?

Describe one way that your daily life will be different because of what you've learned about temptation in this study.

"Lord Jesus, please give me discernment to recognize Your voice and to obey You. Help me not to fall into the grips of temptation and sin, but deliver me from evil. Help me when tested, Lord, to come out as pure gold. Amen."

prayer

a new source of power

The Book of Esther is filled with intrigue, espionage, and romance. The account is basically that of a Miss Universe Pageant where King Xerxes chooses from many beautiful women, one who will serve as his queen.

He chooses Esther, not knowing that her family is living in exile, separated from their Hebrew roots. As the story unfolds, Queen Esther becomes aware of an evil plot against her people by Haman, one of King Xerxes's right-hand men.

What is she to do? If she doesn't go to the king with this information, her people will be destroyed. However, it was highly unusual for even the queen to gain an audience with the king without his invitation. She would take her life into her hands by approaching his throne. If he held out the golden scepter to her, that meant he had given her permission to approach him. If not, the law demanded that she be stoned to death.

Esther and her people fasted and prayed for three days before she made an appearance in the king's court. She even had a terrible fainting spell before entering his presence—either from low blood sugar, stress, or both!

Anyway, as she breathlessly approached the king's throne, each painful step brought her closer to her destiny. Would he extend the scepter and allow her to live, or would he deny her an audience and have her stoned to death?

King Xerxes extended the scepter! She revealed to him the plot against her people and he steped in to save them! Oh, it's a tear-jerker, and one I hope you will read.

King Xerxes was just a human being, reigning over an earthly kingdom. However, you and I have direct access to the King of kings who reigns over worlds seen and unseen! We don't have to fear that He will deny us an audience; in fact, he treasures the moments when we come to Him.

Prayer is really quite simple—it's a two-way dialogue between two people who love each other. Jesus Christ paid the ultimate price on the Cross to give us this direct access.

There is no secret formula for a successful prayer life. All it takes is spending time practicing it each day. You do not have to say certain things a certain way or pray at a certain time of day or for a designated period of time. You just need to speak to God from a sincere heart. As we grow in our faith, prayer becomes our attitude, a constant companion, so that we fulfill the instructions given in 1 Thessalonians 5:16–17: "Be joyful always; *pray continually*; give thanks in all circumstances, for this is God's will for you in Christ Jesus."

Prayer is our power source that acts as a conduit to the Holy Spirit. And when we tap into this power source, our battery never runs low and our tank gage never shows "empty." Praying continues the flow of the Holy Spirit so that we can live supernaturally!

bible study

One of the most impressive things about Jesus Christ's ministry was His prayer life. As we read the accounts of His ministry, we see that He rose early to pray (Mark 1:35), removed Himself from the crowds to pray (Luke 5:16), or was still praying when evening came (Matthew 14:20). If the Son of God—who was perfect in all things—spent that kind of time in prayer, how much more so should we!

Look up these references and describe the situation Jesus was facing before or after His recorded time of prayer. What lessons can we learn?

Matthew 14:13–23

Mark 1:35–39

Matthew 26:36–39

Luke 6:12–26

Luke 5:15–16

Briefly describe the instructions on prayer given to us through the following references:

Matthew 6:5–6

Matthew 6:7–14

Luke 6:27–28

Romans 8:26

Ephesians 6:18

1 Thessalonians 5:16–18

James 5:13–16

1 Peter 4:7

Matthew 26:41

Philippians 4:6–7

Proverbs 15:8, 29

Mark 12:38–40

2 Chronicles 7:14

Matthew 21:12–13; Isaiah 56:6–7

God wants us to come to Him sincere and humble in our confessions and requests. How long does it take God to answer prayer?

Read the account of Abraham's servant in Genesis 24 and compare his situation to that of Paul in 2 Corinthians 12:7 and of Elizabeth and Zechariah in Luke 1:5–20.
What conclusion do you come to?

We have been given clear instructions on how and when to pray as well as a glimpse into the exciting results of prayer. Prayer is a power source for those who know Jesus Christ as their personal Savior and seek to draw closer to Him.

Are there times when our prayers are not heard or answered? Are there conditions to praying? Are there things that hinder our prayers from being answered?

Consider these verses and briefly discuss what the Scriptures reveal about things that can hinder our prayers.

Deuteronomy 1:43, 45

incense in a bowl

The Bible makes it clear how precious are the prayers of the saints. In fact, it appears that they are so precious that God *saves* them!

In Exodus 30, God instructs Aaron, the High Priest, to burn a special blend of incense on the altar in the Tabernacle in the morning and again in the evening.

God often provides a picture, explaining a spiritual truth through a physical example. In Exodus He begins to paint the picture of smoke, representing our prayers, rising from the incense to God. Now if we turn over to Psalm 141:2, we read, "May my prayer be set before you like incense; may the lifting up of my hands be like the evening sacrifice."

We suddenly see a picture of our prayers rising to God like the smoke from the incense! It is a reminder that God hears our prayers and loves the aroma of them.

Now let's turn to Revelation 5:8. Here we are given a vision of the throne room of God. "And when he had taken [the scroll], the four living creatures and the twenty-four elders fell down before the Lamb. Each one had a harp and they were holding golden bowls full of incense, *which are the prayers of the saints.*"

Imagine that! God treasures our prayers so much that as he receives them, they are preserved for all eternity—in bowls of pure gold!

James 1:6

Isaiah 29:13

Psalm 66:18

Hebrews 11:6

Proverbs 8:13

Matthew 6:5–6

Jeremiah 14:10

James 4:3

Prayer is the avenue through which we receive great benefits! Look up the following verses and list areas of blessing we can enjoy when we approach God's throne of grace.

1 John 1:9

Revelation 3:20

Acts 1:24

Psalms 118:5–6; Psalms 23:4

Exodus 33:11

John 14:1

Psalms 68:19

John 14:27; Ephesians 2:14

1 Peter 5:7

John 16:24

Matthew 26:41

James 4:7

Isaiah 40:31

John 3:16

Finally, let's end this lesson on prayer with the beautiful story of Jehoshaphat as told in 2 Chronicles 20.

As the story opens, we find that a "vast army" is about to descend upon the Children of Israel. Their doom and destruction is inevitable. Does Jehoshaphat pace about wildly trying in his own strength to figure out how to protect his people? No! Verse 3 says that first he "inquired of the LORD." Then he asked the people to fast and pray for three days.

Read verses 6–9, one of the most beautiful public prayers in the Bible. Jehoshaphat ends the prayer with a statement we should all memorize and use when we are faced with an insurmountable obstacle: "We do not know what to do, but our eyes are upon you."

Jahaziel, a prophet, then speaks the words of the Lord: "Do not be afraid or discouraged ... *for the battle is not yours but God's.*" Then God instructs Jehoshaphat to fight this battle in an unconventional manner. "Jehoshaphat appointed men to sing to the LORD and praise him ... as they went out at the head of the army: 'Give thanks to the LORD, for his love endures forever.' As they began to sing and praise, the LORD set ambushes against the men ... and they were defeated!"

What a great example to us: inquire of the Lord, fast and pray, sing His praises, and trust Him to guide us. For the battle is not ours but God's!

my plan

To make prayer a part of your daily routine, you've got to plan for it. Here are a few ideas for planning for prayer:

1. *Make an appointment for prayer time, just as you would a doctor's appointment or important meeting. Keep a daily calendar and pencil in appointments with Jesus. If someone calls and wants you to do something at that time, tell them that you have another appointment—a divine one!*

2. *Look for opportunities within your normal daily routine when you can pray as you do something else: pray in the shower, pray while you water the lawn, pray while you're on the treadmill, pray as you clean up the kitchen after supper. Use these normal activities as cues that it's time to pray. You'll soon find yourself with a new habit.*

Some people like a methodical way to pray. Here are a couple of ideas.

1. *Keep a prayer journal. Enter the date at the top and the list of things you want to pray for, or go ahead and actually write out your prayers to God. Either way, your faith will grow when you look back upon your last weeks and months of prayers and see how God has performed miracles in your life!*

2. *Choose a simple format to guide your prayer to be sure you pray in all the ways you want to. A popular format is the "ACTS" method. This a simple acronym prompts*

us to pray in these areas:

Adoration: Adore God for what He is revealing about
Himself to you
Confession: Confess your sins and forgive others as
the Lord is forgiving you.
Thanksgiving: Thank Him for answered prayer and
all the blessings that you enjoy.
Supplication: Make your requests known to the Lord

Choose one or more of thse ideas, or add your own ideas
for developing a habit of prayer here. Set a goal that is real-
istic for you to begin this week:

Sometimes God answers your prayers in astounding way;
other times he may quietly guide you with peace and confidence. Regardless of what the answer and how it is revealed,
we know that there is power when we pray and that prayer
is our power source!

"Father, help me to approach Your throne with boldness
and confidence. Amen."

holy spirit

a new guarantee

After speaking at a conference in Denver for several days, I returned home facing the usual Mom tasks. The boys—dad and sons—did a pretty good job of picking up all evidence of their temporary bachelor lifestyle, but the dishwasher and washing machines had not been run, the dogs' water bowl (that resembles a child's small wading pool) was empty, and the sinks all needed to be hosed down for use by a girl!

Without unpacking, I instinctively started the dishwasher, the washing machine, and proceeded to scrub with soap and water every surface that needed it. My husband and I then shared a nice quiet dinner together and called it an early night since he had a very important out-of-town meeting the next day. He needed to be on the road by 7:00 A.M. I, however, planned to sleep in to get over jet lag!

Well, at 6:30 A.M., my husband sweetly and apologetically woke me up. He was hovering over me wearing an old ski jacket and blue jeans. He had not washed his hair or shaved.

This was not the attire I expected him to wear for his big presentation, so even in my twilight state I knew something was wrong. My husband patiently explained the problem: There was no water.

Our water comes from a well and is brought into the house by a pump in the basement. The pump showed no pressure, yet it seemed to be running correctly. For a short-term solution, we hooked up a hose to our neighbor's outside spigot with the help of a small adapter and were able to tap into their water supply. What a gracious gesture to us at 6:30 in the morning!

Later in the day the repairman showed up, took one look at the pressure gauge on the pump and proceeded to unhook the hose that had delivered the much-needed water from our neighbors. He turned on the water at the kitchen sink and watched the pump work correctly twice. He then pronounced our pump "fixed" and left the bill on the kitchen table. As it turned out, my obsession to clean everything at once using a single water source had depleted the pressure in the pump and it just needed to be primed. Without even realizing it, we had fixed the problem by tapping into our neighbor's water source.

Being filled with the Holy Spirit is a bit like our water dilemma. Yes, when we become born again Christians we are given a portion of the power of the Holy Spirit. But its flow needs to be continually resupplied or we can run out of our power source. So, let's prime our pumps and keep on filling them with the power of the Holy Spirit as we learn about this most important aspect of our new identity in Christ!

bible study

So far, we've studied and learned much about acquiring a new identity in Christ. One thing is for sure—Christianity is more than just head knowledge! When you accepted Christ as your Savior, you were immediately placed into the body of Christ and filled with the Holy Spirit. Second Corinthians 1:21b–22 tells us that "... He (God) anointed us, *set his seal of ownership on us*, and put his Spirit in our hearts as a deposit, guaranteeing what is to come." (See also Ephesians 1:13–14.)

I love this description because I can just visualize God imprinting a stamp of approval on our souls at the moment of salvation. This seal tells Satan, "She's mine! Now that I am living in her, you cannot have her!"

Often people will make a decision for Christ, but then lead a seemingly empty and powerless life. This is because they have failed to tap into the supernatural power of the Holy Spirit. Yes, they have been sealed by and filled with the Holy Spirit, but they must seek an ongoing, growing relationship with Him to realize the strength and power available to them. Some theologians call this the "regenerating power of the Holy Spirit."

Look up the following verses and list the different comforts available to us through the Holy Spirit.

John 16:12–16

John 14:15–21

Romans 14:17

1 Corinthians 2:10-16; 1 John 4:1-6

Galatians 5:22-23

1 Corinthians 12:3-11

Ephesians 1:16-17

The Holy Spirit is part of the Trinity, therefore fully divine. In the following references, describe the divine attributes inherent in the Holy Spirit.

Psalm 139:1-14

Luke 1:35

Hebrews 9:14-15

John 16:7-8

Read Romans 8:1-8. Contrast the differences between those who are living in accordance to the Spirit and those who are not:

Spirit-filled   Sin-filled

1.   1.

2.   2.

3.   3.

4.   4.

Jesus came to this earth to glorify God. In the same way, the Spirit reveals, exalts, and glorifies Jesus. Being filled with the

holy spirit

How can we explain the Trinity—Father, Son, and Holy Spirit? Well, think of good old H_2O and it will clarify the concept.

When we turn on the tap, water comes out. It possesses certain chemical properties that identified it as H_2O.

Take that same water and fill up the ice cube tray. Place it in the freezer overnight and what do you have by morning? Ice! Even though it is in a different form, its chemical properties are still identified as H_2O.

Place some water in your tea kettle and turn up the burner. Soon steam rolls out of the spout. Did the H_2O that you placed in the kettle somehow turn into another property? No! Steam is water in a different form.

It is the same with God the Father, the Son, and the Holy Spirit. All are one yet minister to us in three different dimensions.

Holy Spirit means that we are filled with Jesus Christ.

The Holy Spirit is a person and possesses infinite intellect (2 Corinthians 2:11), a will (2 Corinthians 12:11), and emotion (Romans 15:30). The Spirit possesses all of the divine attributes because He is the Spirit of God.

Psalm 139:7 reveals that the Holy Spirit is omnipresent (present everywhere). 1 Corinthians 2:10–11 tells us that the Holy Spirit is omniscient (all-knowing), and Luke 1:35 assures us that the Holy Spirit is omnipotent (all powerful).

The Greek word used for the Holy Spirit is "paraclete," which when translated means comforter or helper. It is further defined as "one called along beside, one who energizes, strengthens, and empowers." You can see how important our relationship with the Holy Spirit is!

The Holy Spirit was present at the moment of Creation (see Genesis 1:2) and performed certain works throughout the Old Testament and before the ascension of Jesus. Look up the following references and describe briefly the person who was touched by the Holy Spirit and in what way. Note that these particular Scriptures refer to the Holy Spirit *before* the death, burial, and resurrection of Jesus Christ.

Exodus 31:1–5

Who was touched? In what way?

Judges 6:34–40

Who was touched? In what way?

How does "laying out a fleece" apply to our relationship with the Holy Spirit?

Judges 13:24–25

Who was touched? In what way?

1 Samuel 10:9–10

Who was touched? In what way?

1 Samuel 16:1, 13

Who was touched? In what way?

1 Samuel 17:14

Who was touched? In what way?

Matthew 1:18; Luke 1:35

Who was touched? In what way?

Matthew 3:11–17

Who was touched? In what way?

What evidence of the Trinity does this experience reveal?

Matthew 4:1

Who was touched? In what way?

You can read about when the Holy Spirit first came to Jesus' disciples in Acts 1:1–11 and Acts 2:1–4. Then look up these verses to see how the Holy Spirit is described as He works in the lives of believers.

John 14:16

John 14:26

John 16:13; Romans 8:14

Romans 1:4

Romans 8:2

1 Peter 4:14

Revelation 19:10

Romans 8:26

Write a short summary statement that describes who the Holy Spirit is and what powers are made available to you through the work of the Holy Spirit.

my plan

I almost hesitate to end our section on the Holy Spirit by emphasizing danger, but I so want you to be successful in your spiritual walk. For this reason, I want to point out areas where Satan is going to try to get a foothold and keep you from tapping into the power available to you through the Holy Spirit. There is only thing Satan wants more than he wants people not to hear the Word of God, and that is for Christians to live in doubt and powerlessness.

Ephesians 4:30 warns us not to grieve (sadden) the Holy Spirit. Verse 31 then lists things that do this: bitterness, rage, anger, brawling, slander, and malice. First Thessalonians 5:19 points out that it is possible for us to "put out [or quench] the Spirit's fire." That fire working in our hearts is what lets us live in a way that attracts others to the Christian lifestyle and fuels the joy we have in Christ.

How do we avoid grieving and putting out the Spirit's fire? Take a look at the following references and list those things that limit the Spirit's power in our lives:

Isaiah 14:12–14; 1 Peter 5:5

Proverbs 29:25

1 John 2:15–17

Hebrews 11:6

Psalm 44:21; Matthew 5:23–24

Are you wrestling with any of these issues that could possibly be quenching the power of the Holy Spirit in your life? If so, confess those now and pray that you will be released from these things. Remember, the Holy Spirit is totally committed to empowering us to live godly lives. He always stands ready to reassure and comfort us.

And be encouraged! Timothy wrote two centuries ago: "... fan into flame the gift of God ... For God did not give us a spirit of timidity, but a spirit of power, of love and of self-discipline (1 Timothy 1:6–7). That is still true for Christians today!

"Holy Spirit, infuse me with a new infilling of Your power. Amen."

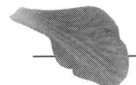

heaven

a new destination

It seems that we all want to end up in heaven, but don't relish the thought of what it takes to get there—dying!

Read and weep with me over the words written by psychologist Jan Bentley: "Someone has said that when we lose a parent we lose the past. When we lose a spouse we lose the present and when we lose a child, we lose the future. That is exactly how I felt as I sat at our kitchen table in the early morning hours of June 22, 1994 and heard the police officer say that our precious daughter, Cheri, our only child, had been involved in a car accident just six miles from our house, and was killed instantly.

"At that moment my dreams and hopes were shattered and in the days and months that followed I experienced the deep pain of living *in the eye of the storm.*

"The journey of grief is not an easy road. Often I prayed desperately that God would hang onto me and help me be obedient to His plan for my life. My courage to go on came only from knowing the character of God and knowing that I can *trust Him.*

"As I look back, through the wisdom of years, I now see—through a rainbow of tears—that I was not in the eye of the storm, but rather I was *in the eye of a miracle.*"

When, through Adam and Eve, sin was introduced into the world, it brought with it thistles, illness, and, yes, death. But the very thing Satan hoped would be the undoing of man, has become the eye of the miracle through which we enter into the perfect presence of a holy God.

If you have received Christ as your personal Savior, your ticket to this eternal paradise has already been printed and issued. At that moment when your soul flees this temporary "tent" which has housed it throughout your lifetime on Earth, the Bible tells us that we will be given a new body—a glorified one that will never die. Imagine that!

Jan and her husband have dealt with their loss because they know the truth about where Cheri is and the process that took her there. Evangelist Billy Graham explained this process in his book, *Angels: God's Secret Agents* (Garden City, NY: Doubleday & Co., 1975, page 75) after witnessing the death of his maternal grandmother. "She sat up in bed and almost laughingly said, 'I see Jesus. He has His arms outstretched toward me. I see Ben (her husband who had died some years earlier) and I see the angels!' She slumped over, absent from the body but present with the Lord." When we have been sealed with the Holy Spirit, death ushers us into the very presence of Jesus and His angels.

This is why the apostle Paul in Philippians 1:21 states that, "To live is Christ and to die is gain." He goes on to say in verse 23 that to be with Christ is "better by far." Yes, Jan will again see her daughter, Cheri, just as we will be reunited with our loved ones in a place that is "better by far!"

bible study

As I write this study, my Aunt Margaret is 80 years old. A retired registered nurse and pastor's wife, she has always maintained that living a life based on the teachings of Jesus would be well worth the commitment—even if there were no afterlife.

God's instruction is what allows us to live our lives in peace and joy and gives purpose to our existence here on Earth. However, I know that Aunt Margaret, edging ever closer to life's precipice, knows the rewards awaiting her in heaven. For one, she will be reunited with her son, John, who passed away of cancer at the age of 45. She will be surrounded with a brilliance she can't even imagine from her earthly perspective. And she will inherit eternal life as promised to those who have trusted Jesus Christ as their Lord and Savior—whose names are listed in the Lamb's Book of Life.

Much of how we imagine heaven comes to us in symbols and pictures painted for our imagination, because we truly cannot fathom it. However, even imagining heaven "as through a glass darkly" is so electrifying it makes our hair stand on end!

Now that you have taken on a new identity—one based upon the work and person of Jesus Christ—you are His bride and stand to inherit unfathomable riches. So take my hand and let me lead you through our last chapter into the very presence of God's throne room and give you a brief glimpse of the home that awaits us—our eternal dwelling place!

Read John 14:1–7.

What has Jesus promised he would do?

How can we get there?

How does Jesus describe Himself?

How does this comfort you?

Read Revelation 4:1–11.

How does John describe the throne room of God in heaven?

What impresses you most about the description?

What purpose does the throne seem to serve?

Note the items that are described as being "like" an earthly familiarity and list them.

Revelation 21 contains a description of the New Jerusalem, a picture of our eternal dwelling place. Read the chapter in its entirety then ponder the following points:

Who is the bride?

Why do you suppose God uses this picture?

In one-word exclamations, describe your impression of the New Jerusalem when you read verses 15–21.

Why is it significant that there will be no Temple in the New Jerusalem (verse 22)?

Who will enter the gates of the New Jerusalem?

Not only will there be a new heaven and a new Earth, but other things will be made new. Look up the following verses and note the things about *us* that will be made new:
Philippians 3:20–21

Isaiah 65:17

1 John 3:2–3

Psalm 37:4

Psalm 51:10

Psalm 40:3

Isaiah 62:2

The Bible spells out the many ways that angels serve God for the glory of His kingdom. In fact, the word "angel" describes their function, which is to be a "messenger."

Read Revelation 7:9–12 and describe the angelic activity in heaven.

How does their activity encourage you?

What other activity will there be in heaven?

heaven—
a place of "no mores"

How does one describe something as unimaginable as heaven? First Corinthians 2:9 tells us that "no eye has seen, no ear has heard, no mind has conceived what God has prepared for those who love him." The only way we can observe an even minute glimpse of heaven is to compare it to something earthly (which pales in significance) or to describe what it is *not.*

Revelation 21 tells us what will not be in heaven:

- No sea
- No death
- No crying
- Nothing impure
- No moon
- No tears
- No mourning
- No pain
- No sun
- No night

Revelation 21 also tells us what will be in heaven: God will be seated on His righteous throne, and His glory will shine so brightly that there will be no need for sun or moon, for God is "making everything new!"

Read Revelation 22, the last chapter of the Bible.

How does John continue his description of heaven? (Notice the role of the angel!)

How does John respond when these things are revealed to him (v. 8)?

What does the angel say? What does this reveal about angels?

What are Jesus' last recorded words in the Bible?

Probably one of the most familiar Bible verses is John 3:16: "For God so loved the world that he gave his one and only Son, that whosoever believes in him shall not perish but have eternal life." This verse so clearly points out the way to receive eternal life. Did you ever wonder what situation preceded these remarks of Jesus? You can read the whole story in John 3:1-21, where Jesus talks to Nicodemus about being born again.

When we're born again we take the first step on a journey that will take us to heaven. Someday, when the end of time comes, Jesus will come again and all of God's people will be gathered to heaven. Throughout His ministry, Jesus often referred to Himself as the shepherd and to those of us who follow Him as His sheep. In John 10:14, Jesus comforts us by saying "I am the good shepherd; I know my sheep and my sheep know me ... and I lay down my life for the sheep."

Jesus encourages us to be ready for His return and uses the teaching of a parable to make His point. In Jesus' time, the bride and her bridesmaids would await the arrival of the groom, not knowing when he would come for his beloved. Therefore, she had to be ready for him at any time during a given period. You can read the story Jesus told in Matthew 25:1–13.

In Philippians 3:20, Paul reminds us that "our citizenship is in heaven." In other words, this earth is not really our home, it is just a passageway to get to our final destination—heaven.

Therefore, we must begin to think of ourselves as those who are alien to this world, and as Colossians 3:1–2 says, "set your hearts on things above, where Christ is seated at the right hand of God. Set your minds on things above, not on earthly things."

This takes a little practice as we pour over unpaid bills and face the challenges of daily living. However, we must put *all* things into eternal perspective. Our citizenship is in heaven, where God makes all things new, and Jesus provides the way for us to go to heaven.

"'Yes, I am coming soon.' Amen. Come, Lord Jesus."

my plan

Our imagination has soared as we've tried to somehow capture and picture what heaven will look like. It is mind-boggling to say the least!

Write down several words that describe how you feel about going to heaven.

Now that you are a Christian, an important aspect of your new identity is to reveal the new "you" to those around you. Walking the Christian life is a process, and over time your outward actions will begin to reflect your inward convictions. However, it's not too early to begin sharing your faith and the truths that you have learned through God's Word.

Take a moment to list the names of those with whom you would like to share your experience.

Once you have prayed for each person, consider ways that you can begin revealing your new-found faith and the truths you've learned. It may be over lunch or at coffee break. It might be a note you drop in the mail. It might be sharing a book and discussing it or inviting your friend to a special event where you'll have an opportunity to talk. In some way, make a commitment to begin sharing what God is doing in your life. Write down some ideas that you are comfortable with.

Then, together, let's pray and ask the Lord to begin working in the heart of those you've shared with so that you can lead them to a saving knowledge of Jesus Christ too!

"Dear Heavenly Father, we come boldly before You asking for opportunity and courage to share with others how they can also enjoy heaven and eternal life with us. Help us to live our lives in such a way that they will want what we have—Your Holy Spirit living in us. Amen."

a final word

W e've just scratched the surface in this Bible study of the foundational concepts of your new-found faith. Oh, how I want you to hunger and thirst after the Word of God and all that it has for you! My prayer is that you will now want to dig deeper and grow stronger in your relationship with Jesus Christ.

Christianity is *not* a religion—it *is* a relationship! It is unique from every other world religion because it is based upon a personal friendship with the only God who is still alive and lives in us today. No other religion or religious leader can make these claims.

Your relationship with Jesus Christ is also going to impact your relationships with those around you. There may be times when this will be frustrating—when others just can't "see" what you see—or it may be overwhelmingly rewarding as you recognize those around you who are also in the family of God! You will want to delve deeper into this reality by using the second Bible study in the Fresh Start series, *My New Relationships in Christ*.

The best closing advice I can share with you is this:

don't give up and don't give in! Now that God has His seal upon you, Satan will try every slick trick he can think of to make you doubt and be discouraged in your faith. He can't touch you! Keep your eyes focused upon God, using prayer as a way to communicate with Him, and keep reading His Holy Word as a way for Him to reply to you. Remember, you have a supernatural power source available to you in the person of the Holy Spirit. Pray daily for a new infilling of His presence and power.

We would love to hear from you as you take these important steps in your spiritual journey. You can connect with us on the web at **www.timeoutforwomen.com**.

Bless, you my dear sister, and let me pray for you as you seek God's truth and will in your life:

"Heavenly Father, thank You so much for giving us Your precious son, Jesus Christ, and for taking the eternal punishment that should have been ours. Holy Spirit, give us a fresh infilling of Your mighty power, and thank You for this fresh start.

"Lord, I pray especially for my sister who has diligently sought You through this Bible study. May the truths of Your Word, Father, come to life and be made real in her life. Guide her, encourage her, and prepare her for service in Your kingdom. We give You all the glory and ask these things in the name of Your son Jesus Christ. 'Amen. Come, Lord Jesus.'"